I0825481

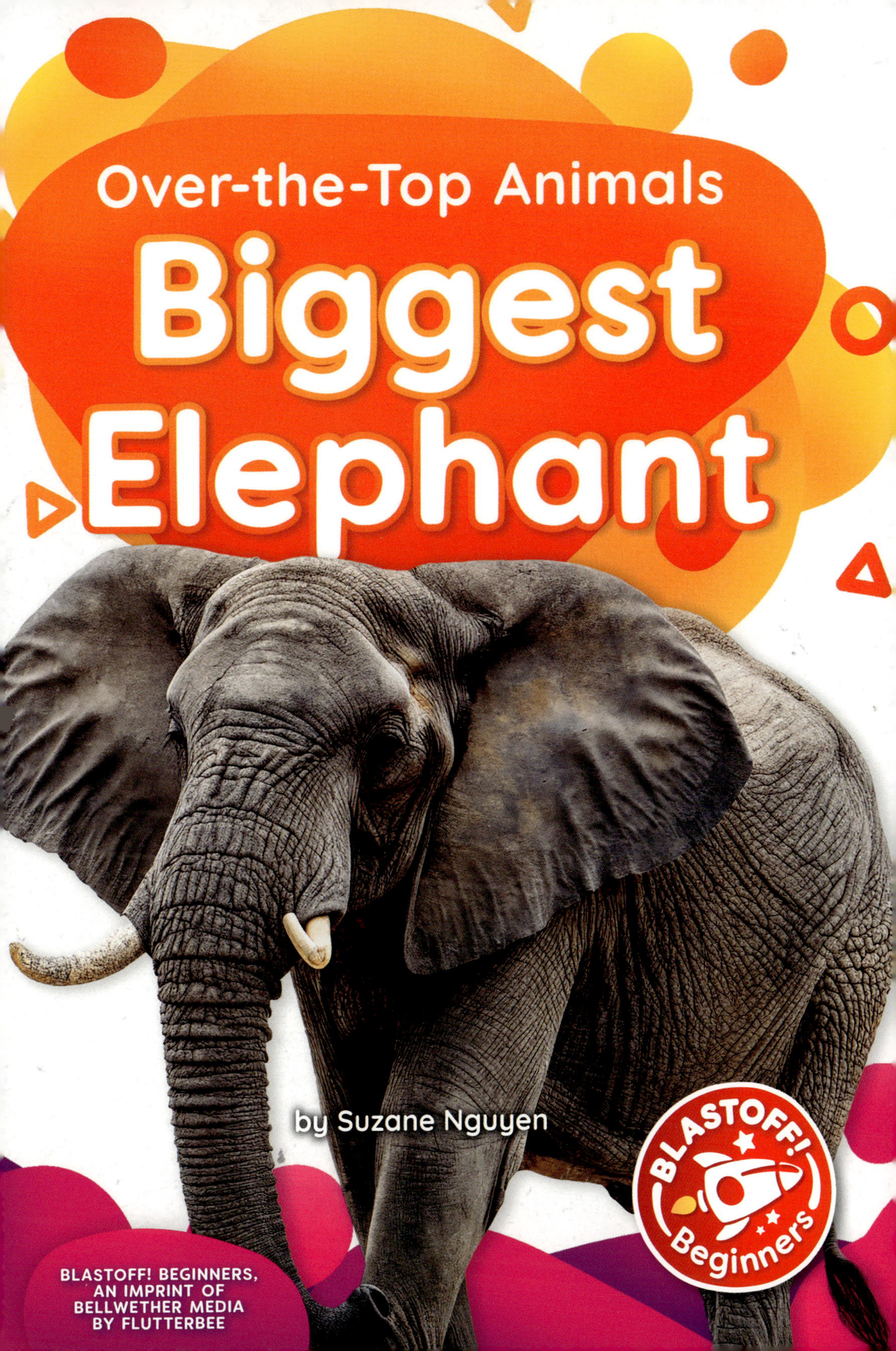

Over-the-Top Animals

Biggest Elephant

by Suzane Nguyen

BLASTOFF! BEGINNERS, AN IMPRINT OF BELLWETHER MEDIA BY FLUTTERBEE

Blastoff! Beginners are developed by literacy experts and educators to meet the needs of early readers. These engaging informational texts support young children as they begin reading about their world. Through simple language and high frequency words paired with crisp, colorful photos, Blastoff! Beginners launch young readers into the universe of independent reading.

Sight Words in This Book

a	can	is	their	with
an	eat	it	these	
and	from	long	they	
are	have	so	use	
big	help	the	water	

This edition first published in 2027 by Bellwether Media, Inc.

Text copyright © 2027 by Bellwether Media, Inc. All rights reserved. No part of this publication may be reproduced, stored in any retrieval system, or transmitted in any form or by any means, electronic, mechanical, photocopying, recording, or otherwise, without written permission of the publisher.

BLASTOFF! BEGINNERS and associated logos are trademarks and/or registered trademarks of Bellwether Media, Inc. Bellwether Media is a division of FlutterBee Education Group.

For information regarding permission, write to Bellwether Media, Inc., Attention: Permissions Department, 3500 American Blvd W, Suite 150, Bloomington, MN 55431.

Library of Congress Cataloging-in-Publication Data is available at www.loc.gov or upon request from the publisher.

ISBN: 9798893049954 (hardcover)
ISBN: 9798898801373 (ebook)

Editor: Betsy Rathburn Designer: Laura Sowers

Printed in the United States of America, North Mankato, MN.

Table of Contents

Super Animals

An African bush elephant eats leaves. It is so big!

Big and Strong

These elephants are huge. They are the biggest land **mammals**!

They have
strong bodies.
They can
push over trees!

They have long **tusks**. They have big ears.

tusk

They have strong **trunks**. They can lift a motorcycle!

trunk

Mighty Giants

These elephants use their size. They dig big water holes.

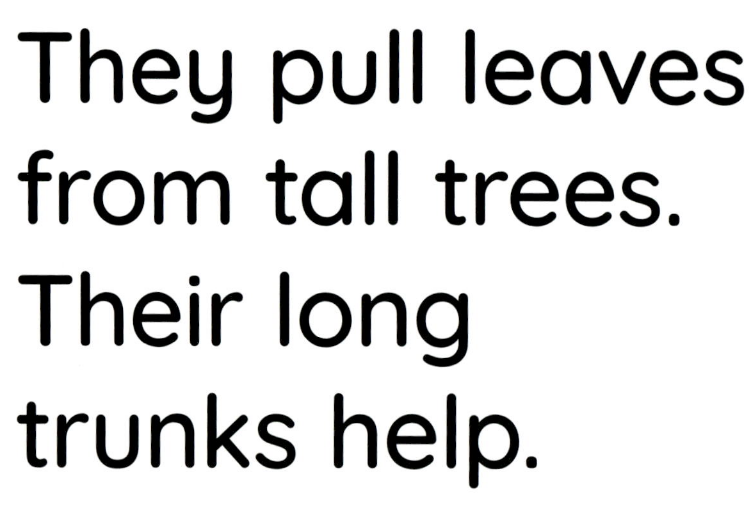

They pull leaves from tall trees. Their long trunks help.

They stay safe.
They fight with
their long tusks.

Elephants are big and strong. They are mighty!

The Biggest Elephant

Body Parts

Using Their Size

dig big water holes

find food

fight

Glossary

mammals

warm-blooded animals that have hair and feed their young milk

trunks

the long noses and upper lips of elephants

tusks

the large teeth of an elephant

To Learn More

ON THE WEB

FACTSURFER

Factsurfer.com gives you a safe, fun way to find more information.

1. Go to www.factsurfer.com.
2. Enter "biggest elephant" into the search box and click 🔍.
3. Select your book cover to see a list of related content.

Index

The images in this book are reproduced through the courtesy of: Hanna, front cover; letr, p. 3; Bim, pp. 4-5; Roger de la Harpe, pp. 6-7; Ulrich Doering, pp. 8-9; Soumabrata Moulick, pp. 10-11; Bernie Olbrich, pp. 12-13; ArCaLu, pp. 14-15; Gemma Campling, pp. 16-17; Rikus Visser, pp. 18-19; LoW MD, p. 20; andreanita, pp. 20-21; photomaster, p. 22; Nick Dale, p. 22 (dig big water holes); art_zzz, p. 22 (find food); Uryadnikov Sergey, p. 22 (fight); John, p. 23 (mammals); phototrip.cz, p. 23 (trunks); James, p. 23 (tusks).